Horns and Forts

Written by Abbie Rushton
Illustrated by Mat Edwards

Collins

cook the food on coals

a short fur coat

a sharp tool cuts wood

cook the food on coals

a short fur coat

a goat with horns

wool on a loom

a goat with horns

wool on a loom

a sharp tool cuts wood

a good fort

a good fort

Review: After reading

Use your assessment from hearing the children read to choose any GPCs, words or tricky words that need additional practice.

Read 1: Decoding
- Use grapheme cards to make any words you need to practise. Model reading those words, using teacher-led blending. Remove the scaffolds as the children become more confident.
- Ask the children to follow as you read the whole book, demonstrating fluency and prosody.
- Turn to pages 10 and 11. Draw the children's attention to the word **wood**. Remind them of the two different sounds that /oo/ can make. Can they find another word with the short /**oo**/ sound? (*good*)

Read 2: Vocabulary
- Look back through the book and discuss the pictures. Encourage the children to talk about details that stand out for them. Use a dialogic talk model to expand on their ideas and recast them in full sentences as naturally as possible.
- Work together to expand vocabulary by naming objects in the pictures that children do not know.
- Turn to page 7 and discuss the meaning of **wool** and **loom**. Point to the loom. Tell the children that a loom is used to weave wool and make cloth. Discuss how the Vikings made their clothes by weaving wool and how we can still weave with wool today.

Read 3: Comprehension
- Turn to pages 2 and 3. Ask: Have you seen or read about a village like this before? Encourage them to talk about whether they would like to live in the village shown in this book and why.
- Tell the children that this book is showing life in the past. It is a history book telling us about Viking life. Go back through the book and encourage the children to talk about what they notice.
- Turn to pages 14 and 15. Encourage the children to name objects in the picture. Prompt with questions such as: What does the goat have? (*horns*) What sort of coat is the man sitting down wearing? (*a fur coat*) What is the woman weaving on the loom? (*wool*)

Published by Collins
An imprint of HarperCollins*Publishers*

The News Building
1 London Bridge Street
London
SE1 9GF
UK

Macken House
39/40 Mayor Street Upper
Dublin 1
D01 C9W8
Ireland

© HarperCollins*Publishers* Limited 2025

Wandle Learning Trust name and logo © Wandle Learning Trust

10 9 8 7 6 5 4 3 2 1

ISBN 978-0-00-875813-4

All rights reserved. No part of this publication may be reproduced, stored in a retrieval system, or transmitted in any form by any means, electronic, mechanical, photocopying, recording or otherwise, without the prior written permission of the Publisher or a licence permitting restricted copying in the United Kingdom issued by the Copyright Licensing Agency Ltd, 5th Floor, Shackleton House, 4 Battle Bridge Lane, London SE1 2HX.

Without limiting the author's and publisher's exclusive rights, any unauthorised use of this publication to train generative artificial intelligence (AI) technologies is expressly prohibited. HarperCollins also exercise their rights under Article 4(3) of the Digital Single Market Directive 2019/790 and expressly reserve this publication from the text and data mining exception.

British Library Cataloguing-in-Publication Data
A catalogue record for this publication is available from the British Library.

Author: Abbie Rushton
Illustrator: Mat Edwards (Advocate Art)
Reading ideas author: Liz Miles
Publisher: Laura White
Product manager: Natasha Paul
Series editor: Charlotte Raby
Phonics consultant: Catherine Baker
Project manager: Emily Hooton
Phonics reviewer: Jacqueline Harris
Proofreader: Gaynor Spry
Designer: 2Hoots Publishing Services Ltd
Production controller: Katharine Willard

Developed in collaboration with Little Wandle Letters and Sounds Revised

Printed in the UK

Get the latest Collins Big Cat news at
collins.co.uk/collinsbigcat

MIX
Paper | Supporting
responsible forestry
FSC™ C007454

This book contains FSC™ certified paper and other controlled sources to ensure responsible forest management.

For more information visit: www.harpercollins.co.uk/green
collins.co.uk/sustainability

Made with responsibly sourced paper and vegetable ink

Scan to see how we are reducing our environmental impact.

Horns and Forts

Phonemes covered:
/oa/ /oo/ /ɑː/ /**oo**/ /o͞o/
/ɜː/

Blending practice

Phase 3
Set 1

Look at cool forts and lots of jobs.

A simple non-fiction book

collins.co.uk/collinsbigcat